Poetry for Young People
William Carlos Williams

Edited by Christopher MacGowan
Illustrations by Robert Crockett

Sterling Publishing Co., Inc.
New York

For Mariel and James
—*C.M.*

ibrary of Congress Cataloging-in-Publication Data

Williams, William Carlos, 1883-1963.
   [Poems. Selections]
   William Carlos Williams : poetry for young people / edited by Christopher
MacGowan ; illustrated by Robert Crockett.
      p. cm.
   Includes index.
   Summary: A collection of thirty poems with illustrations and brief introductory
remarks.
   ISBN 1-4027-0006-7
   1. Young adult poetry, American. [1. American poetry.] I. Title: Poetry for
young people. II. MacGowan, Christopher J. (Christopher John) III. Crockett,
Robert, ill. IV. Title.
PS3545.I544A6 2003
811'.52—dc21
                                                     2003006885

2 4 6 8 10 9 7 5 3 1

Published by Sterling Publishing Co., Inc.
387 Park Avenue South, New York, NY 10016
Text © 2004 by Christopher MacGowan
Illustrations © 2004 by Robert Crockett
Distributed in Canada by Sterling Publishing
%Canadian Manda Group, One Atlantic Avenue, Suite 105
Toronto, Ontario, Canada M6K 3E7
Distributed in Great Britain and Europe by Chris Lloyd at Orca Book
Services, Stanley House, Fleets Lane, Poole BH15 3AJ, England
Distributed in Australia by Capricorn Link (Australia) Pty. Ltd.
P.O. Box 704, Windsor, NSW 2756, Australia

Sterling ISBN 1-4027-0006-7

CONTENTS

INTRODUCTION

William Carlos Williams, one of the most important American poets of the twentieth century, was known to most of the people in the small New Jersey town where he lived all his life as their kindly local doctor. His parents insisted that he concentrate on science, not literature, and in high school he was only a C student. Just four copies of his first book of poems were sold, and he could not find a regular publisher for his work for more than half of his writing career. His poetry won its most important prize when he had been dead four months, an award for a book that he wrote when he was nearly 80 and severely handicapped by a series of heart attacks.

William Carlos was born on September 17, 1883, in Rutherford, New Jersey, then a small but growing suburb of New York City. In his boyhood, farms, not the multi-lane highways that surround it today, bordered the town. There was no gas or electricity, no phone service, no water supply, and no public transport. His parents had settled there in the year that William was born.

His father, William George Williams, had been born in England, but came to the United States at the age of five with his mother, Emily, after his father abandoned them. In America Emily found a new husband and moved with him and her son to Santo Domingo in the Dominican Republic. William George grew up in the Caribbean where he met and wooed his wife, Rachel "Elena" Hoheb, who had grown up in Puerto Rico. This Spanish side of William Carlos's heritage was one he was always very proud of.

Elena was fluent in Spanish, like her husband William George, and also in French, but spoke only broken English, a language she disliked. Growing up in New Jersey, William Carlos heard three languages spoken around the house—Spanish, French, and English. Grandmother Emily was the one who taught him English, for his father was often away, sometimes making long trips to South America and the Caribbean in connection with his work for a perfume company in New York City. When he was home, William George would often keep his two sons spellbound with stories of adventure from his boyhood—exploring the tropical jungles of the Caribbean and experiencing the dangers of earthquakes, hurricanes, and tidal waves. He also read Shakespeare's works aloud to them in the evenings and inspired both of them to act in the local dramatic society. For a while William even thought of becoming a professional actor.

William's brother, Edgar, who in later years became a well-known architect, was only thirteen months younger than the future poet. The two were close, although competitive, as brothers can be. Edgar made the school football team as a first-string halfback, but William had to settle for being an alternate. The most serious disagreement between the two came years later, when they had finished college and both fell in love with the same girl, Charlotte Herman. A shy William Carlos stayed home and asked Edgar to propose marriage for both of them. She chose Edgar, but they later broke their engagement. Meanwhile, William Carlos went on to marry her sister, Florence.

It was with other friends, rather than brother Edgar, that William Carlos explored the wild marshlands surrounding Rutherford, intently studying and memorizing the names of the abundant wildflowers and birds that would later appear in his poetry.

When the boys were 13 and 14 their mother traveled with them to Switzerland where they attended school for a year in order to improve their French. Since most of the other boys at the school wanted to speak English, the plan didn't work. The three returned home from Europe in early 1899, and the brothers began attending the private Horace Mann School in New York City. For three years this meant getting up at six o'clock, gulping down breakfast, dashing for the 7:16 train to the Jersey City ferry (no bridges or tunnels had been built yet across the Hudson River) which took them to downtown Manhattan. Then they would take the elevated train, which had just become electric, to the West Side of the city and take a brisk walk to Morningside Heights for their first class at nine o'clock. This is when Elena decided that her eldest son should study science and take up the same career—medicine—as his namesake, her brother Carlos back in Puerto Rico. Despite William's C average, one teacher did notice his writing talent and years later the poet dedicated a book of essays to him, remembering with affection "the first English teacher who ever gave me an A." Meanwhile, William George offered the boys a dollar for each book they got through from his list of important historical and philosophical works. The books were long and pretty tough going, but the boys took up the challenge and earned some dollars.

In 1902, when he reached nineteen, William entered the freshman class of the University of Pennsylvania, to study medicine. He had agreed to become a doctor, but was not going to give up his passion for literature and knew that he also wanted to write poetry. Mostly he wrote poems that were imitations of his favorite long-dead English poets. These poems used archaic language (birds were called "nestlings," for instance) because it sounded more "poetic." They were about the kinds of subjects that he thought poems ought to be about, such as love, beauty, and nature, and they used rhyme and a regular beat. When he had been at college a few months, a friend told him that he ought to meet another student who was always writing poetry named Ezra Pound. Williams and Pound became lifelong friends, although they sometimes had strong disagreements about poetry and especially about Pound's prejudiced ideas on race. Within a few years Pound settled in London, England, where he helped to start a new way of thinking about poetry. He became one of the most famous and important poets of the century.

After graduation, Williams continued his medical training in New York City, working in one of its poorest districts. He went to visit Ezra Pound in London, and then traveled to Leipzig, Germany, to study pediatric medicine. Just before the trip he published his first book of poems, a pamphlet of only 22 pages. He paid for 200 copies of the book to be printed, calling it *Poems*, and it went on sale at a local newspaper shop in Rutherford. The store sold four copies and earned Williams a grand total of one dollar. He gave a few copies away to friends; then shortly afterward the shed where all the other copies were stored burned down. Years later he wanted to forget that he had ever written such poems, for they were like the "poetic" verses he had been writing in college, and he never allowed most of them to be reprinted.

Williams proudly sent a copy of *Poems* to Ezra Pound in London. Pound replied gently in a letter that while his friend was talented, he was merely writing the kind of poems that had been written many, many times before. Pound sent Williams a reading list of modern poets, and Williams was grateful, but when Pound continued sending lists for the next 50 years, Williams got a little irritated. He would reply asking Pound how much *he* knew about medicine. But Pound found a publisher in London for Williams' next book, *The Tempers*, in 1913. It was very hard to find publishers in America at that time who would take a chance on modern poetry. Even such poets as Robert Frost and T.S. Eliot had trouble getting published in America before they became famous. Pound helped them too. The reason publishers shunned modern poetry was that it often used methods that were different from the familiar ones of rhyme and lines of the same length with a regular beat. Modern writers thought that always making poems rhyme led to a poem having more words than the poem needed, or interfered in other ways with what the poet wanted to say. They thought that a regular rhythmic beat was boring. Modern writers wanted to experiment, to surprise readers.

In 1910 Williams obtained his license and began his medical practice. Two years later, when he married Charlotte's sister, Florence, the couple moved to 9 Ridge Road, in the center of Rutherford, the house where Williams was to live for the rest of his life. He added a room on to the house for his medical office and specialized in treating children (and eventually delivered about 3,000 babies). He could have worked as an expensive specialist in New York City, but he was happy to be a doctor in his hometown. Over the years he became quite critical of some of the leaders of the medical profession, thinking that they kept fees too high and did not always put people first. Williams himself would often treat patients for free if they could not afford to pay, especially during the 1930s when many people were unemployed. Although most of the time he loved his work, and saw that it helped his writing be about real lives, he was sometimes frustrated that at the end of the day, when he wanted to write, he would be exhausted from office hours, surgery, and hospital visits.

William and Florence had two sons, William Eric, born in 1913, who also became a doctor and took over his father's practice when he retired, and Paul Herman, born in 1916, who went on to become a businessman.

Some of Williams' new writer friends wondered why he wanted to live in a small town, instead of in a city where he would have lots of opportunities to meet and discuss the latest ideas about poetry with other writers. Pound told Williams many times that he should move to Europe. But as you will see from the poems in this book, Williams thought there was plenty to write about in his own house and garden, in the people and places he saw on his medical rounds, and on the streets of Rutherford and nearby towns and cities. And anyway, New York City was just twenty minutes away by bus or train now that the bridges had been built. He would go there on his afternoon off and visit the latest art shows and meet other writers.

Williams was always interested in painting. He said that he might have become a painter instead of a poet if a doctor could carry an easel and palette around with him. Instead, being a writer, he could jot down incidents and ideas for poems on spare prescription pads that he kept in his car, or between seeing patients in his office. So he was especially interested when Pound told him around 1912 about a new kind of poetry called "Imagism" that borrowed some ideas from painting. Imagism claimed that poetry should express clearly and with no wasted words whatever feeling or object the poem was about. There was no need for a regular beat, or for rhyme; that was artificial and old-fashioned. Imagist poems were short. One of the most famous, Pound's "In a Station of the Metro," is just two lines long. This way of thinking about poems was just what Williams wanted. He could write poems that were like pictures, about his own world of New Jersey—American poems about America that did not have to follow archaic European rules. He would look closely at the landscape around him, just as he had as a boy when he had closely studied the flowers and the wildlife of the marshes, and just as he did as a doctor, when he looked closely at a child in order to diagnose an illness. He began to write poems that used the principles of Imagism. They often present a picture, but they are not as simple as they seem. That is the challenge and excitement of reading them.

Williams did not have to try to make money from his writing, thanks to his income as a doctor. He was free to write whatever he liked and how he liked. When book publishers and magazines rejected his poems, Williams and his friends started their own poetry magazine. They used their own money to pay for it, and for their books to be published, although sometimes they persuaded sympathetic wealthy people to contribute to the costs.

Williams felt isolated and disappointed when in the 1920s many American artists went to live, write, and paint in Europe, where it had become very cheap to live for those with American dollars. To make matters worse, as Williams saw it, the American writer T.S. Eliot, living in London, published the famous poem *The Waste Land*, which was all the things that Williams thought a modern American poem should not be. Set in London, it was gloomy and pessimistic, full of obscure quotations in equally obscure languages, and even included notes telling the reader what books to read (European, not American, books) in order to understand the poem. Williams was more determined than ever to write about American things in America. Over the next twenty years he published poems, short stories, novels—and even a history book that said America had never really declared independence from England in literature. Many other writers greatly admired his work, but relatively few copies of his books were printed or sold. Williams often felt frustrated, especially when readers would write that they could not find copies of his books in any stores.

Two things happened around 1950, when Williams was close to retiring as a doctor, that made him famous. He published a long poem called *Paterson* named after the New Jersey city just outside New York. Paterson is only a few miles from Rutherford, and unlike Rutherford had what he needed for his poem, a long and colorful history. Many of the first factories in the United States had been built there. What made Paterson such a good site was the waterpower from Paterson Falls, the most powerful waterfall in the East after Niagara Falls. Williams put the waterfall at the center of his poem—standing both as landscape exploited for profit, and as a kind of permanent presence that outlasted the factories and the sometimes violent history of the city. The poem ended up more than 250 pages long. *Paterson* is in some parts like a scrapbook or collage, but instead of obscure quotations from European books, Williams inserted letters from his friends, scraps of history, items from newspapers, gossip, conversations he had overheard, and even one of Ezra Pound's irritating reading lists. The poem was much admired and gained lots of attention.

The other important thing that got Williams' work noticed was that by 1950 many younger poets agreed with him that American poetry ought to be about America, and did not need to follow English rules. Many of them visited Williams in Rutherford for advice, or wrote to him. He began to get hundreds of letters, not only from poets and readers, but also from patients and former patients. He always tried to reply. The small New Jersey town suddenly realized their local doctor was a celebrity.

Williams was now invited to give readings and teach poetry all over the country, but he could not do as much as he wanted because he began to have a series of heart attacks that made him more and more frail. He kept on with his poems, but his sight got worse and he had trouble reading. Finally at the age of 78 he had to give up writing. His last poem was about his always excitable dog, Stormy. He died peacefully in his sleep in 1963 and is buried in Rutherford. A few months later his last book of poems, *Pictures from Brueghel*, published in 1962, won the important Pulitzer Prize for Poetry.

Williams has remained a major influence on many American poets, and American poetry would certainly not be what it is today if had not been for the doctor from Rutherford.

THE FOOL'S SONG

Williams copies the kind of merry song that a fool (sometimes called a clown or a jester) would sing in plays written in Shakespeare's time, 400 years ago. The fool's song entertained his master, often a king, but also taught a lesson. Here the lesson is that we should be careful about thinking too quickly that we have captured Truth, for things are often more complicated than we realize.

I tried to put a bird in a cage.
      O fool that I am!
   For the bird was Truth.
Sing merrily, Truth: I tried to put
      Truth in a cage!

And when I had the bird in the cage,
      O fool that I am!
   Why, it broke my pretty cage.
Sing merrily, Truth: I tried to put
      Truth in a cage!

And when the bird was flown from the cage,
      O fool that I am!
   Why, I had nor bird nor cage.
Sing merrily, Truth: I tried to put
      Truth in a cage!
   Heigh-ho! Truth in a cage.

STILLNESS

The loneliness of the poet is like the loneliness of the surrounding landscape, made all the more so as he thinks of the sleeping townsfolk warm in their beds under the snow-covered roofs. In the last line he accepts his isolation, and does not disturb the stillness.

Heavy white rooves
of Rutherford
sloping west and east
under the fast darkening sky:

What have I to say to you
that you may whisper it to them
in the night?

Round you
is a great smouldering distance
on all sides
that engulfs you
in utter loneliness.

Lean above their beds tonight
snow covered rooves;
listen;
feel them stirring warmly within
and say—nothing.

rooves—*an alternative spelling of the plural roofs*
Rutherford—*the New Jersey town where the poet lived and worked*
smouldering—*usually used of a smoky fire, here suggesting the gray light*
  of the dark sky combined with the snow

CHINESE NIGHTINGALE

A typical "imagist" poem, short and like a picture. Sam Wu worked in a local Chinese laundry. This is particularly appropriate here because imagism borrowed some ideas from ancient Chinese and Japanese poetry, especially from the Japanese "haiku," an unrhymed poem that always has three lines.

Long before dawn your light
Shone in the window, Sam Wu;
You were at your trade.

Nightingale—*a nocturnal songbird*

SPRING STRAINS

Celebration of spring is another traditional subject for poetry. The focus here is on movement. The energy of the sun and the sky seem almost to be pulling the trees up from their roots. The birds, whose playful circling connects the trees, the sky, and the sun, supply a frantic energy of their own to the whole scene.

In a tissue-thin monotone of blue-grey buds
crowded erect with desire against
the sky—
      tense blue-grey twigs
slenderly anchoring them down, drawing
them in—

      two blue-grey birds chasing
a third struggle in circles, angles,
swift convergings to a point that bursts
instantly!

      Vibrant bowing limbs
pull downward, sucking in the sky
that bulges from behind, plastering itself
against them in packed rifts, rock blue
and dirty orange!

                                  But—
(Hold hard, rigid jointed trees!)
the blinding and red-edged sun-blur—
creeping energy, concentrated
counterforce—welds sky, buds, trees,
rivets them in one puckering hold!
Sticks through! Pulls the whole
counter-pulling mass upward, to the right,
locks even the opaque, not yet defined
ground in a terrific drag that is
loosening the very tap-roots!

On a tissue-thin monotone of blue-grey buds
two blue-grey birds, chasing a third,
at full cry! Now they are
flung outward and up—disappearing suddenly!

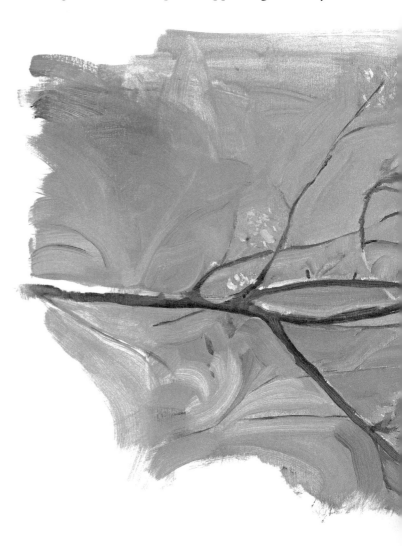

convergings—*coming together from different directions*

rifts—*a term from geology, a series of narrow cracks or fissures in rock*

counterforce—*an opposing force or movement*

puckering—*gathering together in folds or wrinkles*

opaque—*something that light cannot pass through*

tap-roots—*the main, usually center, root of a plant*

DAWN

Celebration of dawn's quiet beauty is another traditional subject in many poems, but this poem is not quiet. It is bursting with energy with all its action and sound words. It has a verb in almost every line.

Ecstatic bird songs pound
the hollow vastness of the sky
with metallic clinkings—
beating color up into it
at a far edge,—beating it, beating it
with rising, triumphant ardor,—
stirring it into warmth,
quickening in it a spreading change,—
bursting wildly against it as
dividing the horizon, a heavy sun
lifts himself—is lifted—
bit by bit above the edge
of things,—runs free at last
out into the open—! lumbering
glorified in full release upward—
　　　　songs cease.

ardor—*with great warmth or passion*

14

LE MÉDICIN MALGRÉ LUI

The title is the same as that of a famous 17th Century French comedy by the playwright Molière. It is about a woodcutter who pretends to be a doctor. As a doctor, Williams humorously mocks himself for not doing what people think a doctor should do—be tidy and look important. The short lines make the poem read like a long, long list of things to do.

Oh I suppose I should
wash the walls of my office
polish the rust from
my instruments and keep them
definitely in order
build shelves in the laboratory
empty out the old stains
clean the bottles
and refill them, buy
another lens, put
my journals on edge instead of
letting them lie flat
in heaps—then begin
ten years back and
gradually
read them to date
cataloguing important
articles for ready reference.
I suppose I should
read the new books.
If to this I added
a bill at the tailor's
and at the cleaner's
grew a decent beard
and cultivated a look
of importance—
Who can tell? I might be
a credit to my Lady Happiness
and never think anything
but a white thought!

"Le Médicin Malgré Lui"—*The Physician in Spite of Himself*

THE LATE SINGER

This was the opening poem in Williams' book Sour Grapes. *Beginning a book of poems with the coming of spring is a tradition that goes as far back as the 1300s. A famous example from that time is Chaucer's great series of poems* The Canterbury Tales.

Here it is spring again
and I still a young man!
I am late at my singing.
The sparrow with the black rain on his breast
has been at his cadenzas for two weeks past:
What is it that is dragging at my heart?
The grass by the back door
is stiff with sap.
The old maples are opening
their branches of brown and yellow moth-flowers.
A moon hangs in the blue
in the early afternoons over the marshes.
I am late at my singing.

cadenzas—*a musical term for a passage inserted into a*
    piece of music especially to display the skills of the
    soloist
moth-flowers—*here probably honeysuckle, sometimes*
    called a moth-flower

WILLOW POEM

The willow tree is often a symbol of sadness in poetry, but here, through careful observation Williams celebrates the tree for the sake of its own beauty.

It is a willow when summer is over,
a willow by the river
from which no leaf has fallen nor
bitten by the sun
turned orange or crimson.
The leaves cling and grow paler,
swing and grow paler
over the swirling waters of the river
as if loath to let go,
they are so cool, so drunk with
the swirl of the wind and of the river—
oblivious to winter,
the last to let go and fall
into the water and on the ground.

THE GREAT FIGURE

Sometimes Williams wrote about what he saw when visiting nearby New York City. In the flash of the moment his eye catches the number of a passing fire truck. This poem became the subject of a well-known painting by Williams' friend the American artist Charles Demuth (1883-1935), which is now prominently displayed in the Metropolitan Museum of Art in New York City.

Among the rain
and lights
I saw the figure 5
in gold
on a red
firetruck
moving
tense
unheeded
to gong clangs
siren howls
and wheels rumbling
through the dark city.

firetruck—*"fire truck" is the more common spelling, but by using the more unusual form the poet speeds up the poem.*

BLIZZARD

The poet imagines a man trekking through a blizzard, but the surprise is that as well as looking back on his tracks in the snow-filled landscape, the man looks back on the journey of his sixty years of life. The poem describes both landscapes at once.

Snow:
years of anger following
hours that float idly down—
the blizzard
drifts its weight
deeper and deeper for three days
or sixty years, eh? Then
the sun! a clutter of
yellow and blue flakes—
Hairy looking trees stand out
in long alleys
over a wild solitude.
The man turns and there—
his solitary tracks stretched out
upon the world.

THE DARK DAY

A poem about threes—even the title has three words in it. Three days of rain is like endless "talking, talking, talking." It seems that it will rain forever, with nothing else to look forward to, only "backward, backward, backward." The three short sentences in the middle (line six) sum up the mood that the rain brings—everyone huddled in upon themselves.

A three-day-long rain from the east—
an interminable talking, talking
of no consequence—patter, patter, patter.
Hand in hand little winds
blow the thin streams aslant.
Warm. Distance cut off. Seclusion.
A few passers-by, drawn in upon themselves,
hurry from one place to another.
Winds of the white poppy! there is no escape!—
An interminable talking, talking,
talking . . . it has happened before.
Backward, backward, backward.

interminable—*tiresome and apparently unending*
seclusion—*solitary, set apart*
Winds of the white poppy—*the white poppy is the source of the drug opium, and of a number of pain-killing and sleep-producing medicines.*

21

PRIMROSE

The variety of wildflowers in the surrounding countryside interested and excited Williams from his boyhood onward. Here the color of the flower begins a rush of past and present memories of the season. There is no grand conclusion to the poem, it ends with just one more detail like all the others. "It is summer!" the third line exclaims, and the poem doesn't let summer end.

Yellow, yellow, yellow, yellow!
It is not a color.
It is summer!
It is the wind on a willow,
the lap of waves, the shadow
under a bush, a bird, a bluebird,
three herons, a dead hawk
rotting on a pole—
Clear yellow!
It is a piece of blue paper
in the grass or a threecluster of
green walnuts swaying, children
playing croquet or one boy
fishing, a man
swinging his pink fists
as he walks—
It is ladysthumb, forget-me-nots
in the ditch, moss under
the flange of the carrail, the
wavy lines in split rock, a
great oaktree—
It is a disinclination to be
five red petals or a rose, it is
a cluster of birdsbreast flowers
on a red stem six feet high,
four open yellow petals
above sepals curled
backward into reverse spikes—
Tufts of purple grass spot the
green meadow and clouds the sky.

ladysthumb—*a plant having clusters of very small, pink flowers*
flange—*a protruding edge or rim*
carrail—*railroad or streetcar rails*
birdsbreast flowers—*flowers pollinated by the action of birds seeking nectar*
sepals—*the leaf-like outer protective covering of a flower*

LIGHT HEARTED WILLIAM

A rare spring-like day comes in November, and makes the poet light hearted. He invents moustaches for himself (he was always clean-shaven) and in the spirit of spring imagines them to be green.

Light hearted William twirled
his November moustaches
and, half dressed, looked
from the bedroom window
upon the spring weather.

Heigh-ya! sighed he gaily
leaning out to see
up and down the street
where a heavy sunlight
lay beyond some blue shadows.

Into the room he drew
his head again and laughed
to himself quietly
twirling his green moustaches.

moustaches—*the plural and "twirling"*
suggest that these are large, even comical

23

SPRING AND ALL

Driving to a nearby hospital, the poet realizes that although the marshy landscape looks as if it is still in the grip of winter, the miracle of spring has just begun. The poem is more generally about birth—babies "enter the new world naked"—also spring is overcoming the winter that is associated with the contagious hospital, "fallen / patches of water," and "dead, brown leaves." Spring is only "lifeless in appearance," but is actually coming alive. The description moves carefully downward, from sky to earth and the awakening roots.

By the road to the contagious hospital
under the surge of the blue
mottled clouds driven from the
northeast—a cold wind. Beyond, the
waste of broad, muddy fields
brown with dried weeds, standing and fallen

patches of standing water
the scattering of tall trees

All along the road the reddish
purplish, forked, upstanding, twiggy
stuff of bushes and small trees
with dead, brown leaves under them
leafless vines—

Lifeless in appearance, sluggish
dazed spring approaches—

They enter the new world naked,
cold, uncertain of all
save that they enter. All about them
the cold, familiar wind—

Now the grass, tomorrow
the stiff curl of wildcarrot leaf

One by one objects are defined—
It quickens: clarity, outline of leaf

But now the stark dignity of
entrance—Still, the profound change
has come upon them: rooted, they
grip down and begin to awaken

the contagious hospital—*a hospital that treats
    contagious diseases (ones that can be spread by contact)*
mottled—*spotted or blotched*
wildcarrot—*usually wild carrot, also called Queen Anne's
    Lace. Here and elsewhere in his poems Williams runs words
    together as if to make the one compound word stand for the
    single object.*

THE FARMER

The farmer is like a poet, for in his imagination he can foresee spring, summer, and fall despite the rain, the mud, and the cold March wind. Both farmer and poet battle blankness (blank fields and blank paper) as they compose their particular harvest, whether a field rich in crops, or a poem.

The farmer in deep thought
is pacing through the rain
among his blank fields, with
hands in pockets,
in his head
the harvest already planted.
A cold wind ruffles the water
among the browned weeds.
On all sides
the world rolls coldly away:
black orchards
darkened by the March clouds—
leaving room for thought.
Down past the brushwood
bristling by
the rainsluiced wagonroad
looms the artist figure of
the farmer—composing
—antagonist

brushwood—*dense undergrowth, or cut or broken-off branches*
rainsluiced—*full of channels caused by the rain*
antagonist—*one who competes with (or opposes) another*

THE RED WHEELBARROW

Williams said that he often saw the wheelbarrow and chickens of this famous poem in a poor neighbor's garden. By making these ordinary objects and their relationship to each other the subject of the whole poem, the poet helps us to recognize how important they are for the neighbor.

so much depends
upon

a red wheel
barrow

glazed with rain
water

beside the white
chickens

27

Williams' house was a short distance from the railroad tracks. He uses onomatopoeia (words that sound like what they refer to) and repetition to capture the slow passing of the freight train and its jostling cars. The poems of earlier times were often like songs, but here a modern machine supplies the music.

To freight cars in the air

all the slow
    clank, clank
    clank, clank
moving above the treetops

the
    wha,   wha
of the hoarse whistle

    pah   pah   pah
    pah, pah, pah, pah, pah

28

piece and piece
piece and piece
moving still trippingly
through the morningmist

long after the engine
has fought by
and disappeared

in silence
to the left

Perhaps here the poet saw the billboard and decided to pull over to a roadside lamp to begin work on this poem. This is a poem about light—the stars, the moon, the lamp, and the advertisement—and also the things they light up, far and near, large and small, mysterious and ordinary, including the poem itself.

The moon, the dried weeds
and the Pleiades—

Seven feet tall
the dark, dried weedstalks
make a part of the night
a red lace
on the blue milky sky

Write—
by a small lamp

the Pleiades are almost
nameless
and the moon is tilted
and halfgone

And in runningpants and
with ecstatic, aesthetic faces
on the illumined
signboard are leaping
over printed hurdles and
"¼ of their energy comes from bread"

two
gigantic highschool boys
ten feet tall

the Pleiades—*a cluster of stars in the constellation*
Taurus, of which six are brightly visible
signboard—*a billboard*
aesthetic—*artistic or beautiful*
(contrasted playfully here with "athletic")
illumined—*lit*

TREE

Although the first words point up the tree's stiffness, the poem is all about the movement that the tree inspires in others with its shape and blossoms. But nothing really changes the tree, not even losing a branch, and the poem returns, like the tree, to where it began.

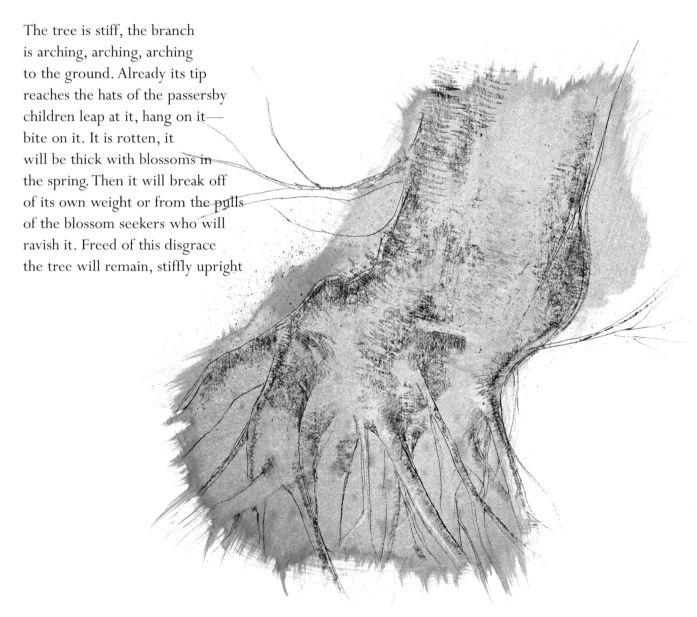

The tree is stiff, the branch
is arching, arching, arching
to the ground. Already its tip
reaches the hats of the passersby
children leap at it, hang on it—
bite on it. It is rotten, it
will be thick with blossoms in
the spring. Then it will break off
of its own weight or from the pulls
of the blossom seekers who will
ravish it. Freed of this disgrace
the tree will remain, stiffly upright

ravish—*seize and carry away by force*

31

POEM

The cat moves across the top of the cupboard step by careful step. Just as every single step is equally important to the cat's successful maneuver, so the short lines of the poem stress almost every word equally.

As the cat
climbed over
the top of

the jamcloset
first the right
forefoot

carefully
then the hind
stepped down

into the pit of
the empty
flowerpot

jamcloset—*a cupboard reserved for storing, often homemade, jams and jellies*

THIS IS JUST TO SAY

Williams thought that what a poem had "to say" did not have to be about grand feelings or major events, but could be about the moments of ordinary, everyday life, like this message from Williams to his wife. We can almost taste and enjoy the plums along with the poet. There are no superfluous words, and the title even serves as the poem's first line: This is Just to Say...

I have eaten
the plums
that were in
the icebox

and which
you were probably
saving
for breakfast

Forgive me
they were delicious
so sweet
and so cold

*icebox—before refrigerators, an insulated
chest or box kept cool by ice*

LATE FOR SUMMER WEATHER

The title suggests that the carefree rambling of this couple, apparently unconcerned at being lost, and almost dancing along the street, is a sight one would expect more in the hot, lazy vacation days of summer than in the early fall.

He has on
an old light grey Fedora
She a black beret

He a dirty sweater
She an old blue coat
that fits her tight

Grey flapping pants
Red skirt and
broken down black pumps

Fat   Lost   Ambling
nowhere through
the upper town they kick

their way through
heaps of
fallen maple leaves

still green—and
crisp as dollar bills
Nothing to do. Hot cha!

Fedora—*a soft felt hat*
pumps—*low-cut shoes, without fastenings*
Hot cha—*A fast Latin American ballroomdance for couples,*
first popular in the 1930s when this poem was written, and
also the title of a 1932 Broadway show. But here it probably
means just "wow!"

BETWEEN WALLS

A poem that does not rhyme has the freedom to point to what is important in a scene by where it places particular details. The important words, "shine," "broken," and "green" (the one splash of color in the poem), come at the end of a line. "Broken" also completes a stanza, as do the single words "cinders" and "bottle." This emphasis happens in the second half of the poem, when the shining glass takes the place of the flowers that, in the first half, we are told cannot grow.

the back wings
of the

hospital where
nothing

will grow lie
cinders

in which shine
the broken

pieces of a green
bottle

PERFECTION

Williams wanted his readers to look everywhere for beauty, not just in the usual places. This poem is a careful description of unexpected loveliness. One part of the "perfection" is that it has been created entirely and only by the poet and by nature. The poet put the apple on the porch rail himself, and "No one. No one!" has moved it since.

O lovely apple!
beautifully and completely
            rotten,
hardly a contour marred—

        perhaps a little
shrivelled at the top but that
            aside perfect
in every detail! O lovely

        apple! what a
deep and suffusing brown
            mantles that
unspoiled surface! No one

        has moved you
since I placed you on the porch
            rail a month ago
to ripen.

        No one. No one!

suffusing—*spread through or over*
mantles—*covers*

36

THE STORM

The poem is a single sentence. Apart from the exclamation mark following and setting apart the surprise of the rainbow, no punctuation interrupts the flow of the various details as they interact to produce the dramatic contrasts of the scene.

A perfect rainbow! a wide
arc low in the northern sky
spans the black lake

troubled by little waves
over which the sun
south of the city shines in

coldly from the bare hill
supine to the wind which
cannot waken anything

but drives the smoke from
a few lean chimneys streaming
violently southward

supine—*sloping*
the city—*New York City, whose skyline*
   can be seen above the horizon from across the New
    Jersey marshlands

FROM *PATERSON*

Williams originally published his long poem Paterson *in four books, and these lines are from the end of what was to be the fourth and last book. He once wrote that the man heading inland was meant to be the famous 19th Century poet Walt Whitman. Williams greatly admired the fact that Whitman did not write according to the rules of poetry from England, but in his own way and about American things. For Williams, genuine American poetry began with Whitman, and therefore this original ending of* Paterson *returns to what, for Williams, was an imagined new beginning for American poetry. However, a few years later Williams added a fifth book, and later still had written a few pages of a sixth before illness forced him to give up writing. This work would always remain "in progress" and was never to have a final ending.*

Wiping his face with his hand he turned
to look back to the waves, then
knocking at his ears, walked up
to stretch out flat on his back in
the hot sand   .   there were some
girls, far down the beach, playing ball.

—must have slept. Got up again, rubbed
the dry sand off and walking a
few steps got into a pair of faded
overalls, slid his shirt on overhand (the
sleeves were still rolled up) shoes,
hat where she had been watching them under
the bank and turned again
to the water's steady roar, as of a distant
waterfall   .   Climbing the
bank, after a few tries, he picked
some beach plums from a low bush and
sampled one of them, spitting the seed out,
then headed inland, followed by the dog.

some girls far down the
      beach—*Williams' detail refers to
      a famous scene in Homer's epic poem*
      The Odyssey, *when the hero Ulysses is
      wakened by girls playing ball at the beach.*
overhand—*with the hands above the shoulder*
a distant waterfall—*the 77 feet (23m) high,
      280 feet (84m) wide Great Falls of Paterson
      is the second largest waterfall by volume
      (after Niagara Falls) east of the Mississippi. It
      is an important symbol in the poem.*

THE BANNER BEARER

The poem matches the dog's hurried four-footed stride by putting emphasis on almost every word in the short, four-line stanzas. Breaking up long words to stress every syllable contributes to this effect. The title playfully calls the dog a "banner bearer" as if he is carrying a banner (his high, straight tail?) at the head of an army or a parade "going into new territory." But the lonesome dog in the rain has his own obscure purposes.

In the rain, the lonesome
dog idiosyn-
cratically, with each
quadribeat, throws

out the left fore-
foot beyond
the right intent, in
his stride,

on some obscure
insistence—from bridge-
ward going
into new territory.

idiosyncratically—*in his own way, special to him*
quadribeat—*four beats*
bridgeward—*towards the bridge*

THE MOTOR-BARGE

In the 1940s canal-barges were still being used to move loads that would now go by truck. The pauses, caused by the punctuation and the line breaks, mimic the slow but determined movement of the barge through the packed, broken ice and the thick, heavy air that is like "lead."

The motor-barge is
at the bridge the
air lead
the broken ice

unmoving. A gull,
the eternal
gull, flies as
always, eyes alert

beak pointing
to the life-giving
water. Time
falters but for

the broad river-
craft which
low in the water
moves grad-

ually, edging
between the smeared
bulkheads,
churning a mild

wake, laboring
to push past
the constriction
with its heavy load

bulkheads—*the upright partitions on a ship dividing it into sections or compartments*
wake—*the track or turbulence left by a ship in the water as it moves*
constriction—*an impediment making an area narrower or smaller by shrinking or contracting*

THE PROBLEM

This poem was written after the poet's serious heart problems began, forcing him to retire from medicine. His questions about the old church could also have been about his own life. How would he survive surrounded by a changing modern world? He put faith in his own "materials," perhaps his failing body as well as his writing. Williams wrote a number of poems in this three-step line pattern in his last books. He claimed that the differing line lengths and resulting pauses represented special characteristics of American speech.

How to fit
   an old brownstone church
      among a group
of modern office buildings:
   The feat stands,
      so that the argument
must be after the fact.
   We can learn from it
      how—
if it is not too late—
   to conduct
      our lives.
Unlike the Acropolis,
   on which there is
      no destructive pressure
but time,
   this building
      is threatened
from all sides.
   What is it
      that has made
its fragile masonry,
   four-square,
      simple in design
so comparatively
   indestructible?
      It does not lodge,
per se,
   in the materials.
      Yet,

that is,
      precisely,
            the point. Where else,
if not in the materials,
      does it lodge?
            Strong forces,
not necessarily of evil,
      are involved.
            But this building
peacefully
      stands.
            Witness merely how
in the morning light
      it preserves itself,
            how confidently,
and without strain,
      it faces the world.
            As if,
and indeed it is so,
      should it be tumbled down,
            nothing
could replace it.

brownstone—*brownish-red sandstone*
the Acropolis—*the high fortified area in Athens,*
    Greece, containing the Parthenon and other
    buildings
masonry—*stonework or brickwork*
per se—*(Latin) in or by itself*

IRIS

The "burst of iris" that wakens the household to breakfast combines smell, color, and most importantly here, sound, as the "trumpeting petals" send forth their music.

a burst of iris so that
come down for
breakfast

we searched through the
rooms for
that

sweetest odor and at
first could not
find its

source then a blue as
of the sea
struck

startling us from among
those trumpeting
petals

44

POEM

Many poems celebrate the rose, but this one celebrates a poem about a rose, and is therefore titled "Poem." "Save" means two things at the beginning of the second stanza. One meaning is "except," but the other tells us that the rose is saved from the cycle of nature by the poem's praise. In nature, the rose must fade to produce the seed, but in the poem the seed is the unfaded rose itself.

The rose fades
and is renewed again
by its seed, naturally
but where

save in the poem
shall it go
to suffer no diminution
of its splendor

diminution—*the act or process of making
smaller*

45

HEEL & TOE TO THE END

The Soviet astronaut Yuri Gagarin was the first man to circle the earth in space. Newspaper reports of the event quoted Gagarin as saying he joyfully "floated, ate, and sang" while in orbit, and Williams puts the words directly into the poem. The term "measure" applies to mathematics, but also to dance steps, and to the rhythm of a poem. In using it, Williams, like Gagarin, turns a scientific achievement (all that division and subtraction) into the sheer exuberance of artistic expression and the joy of being alive.

Gagarin says, in ecstasy,
he could have
gone on forever

he floated
ate and sang
and when he emerged from that

one hundred eight minutes off
the surface of
the earth he was smiling

heel and toe—*putting his feet together as in dance steps*

Then he returned
to take his place
among the rest of us

from all that division and
subtraction a measure
toe and heel

heel and toe he felt
as if he had
been dancing